SECRETS OF SLIME
RECIPE BOOK

30 PROJECTS FOR STRETCHABLE, SQUISHY, SENSORY FUN!

JACKIE HOUSTON
PHOTOGRAPHY BY MARIJA VIDAL

ROCKRIDGE
PRESS

For general information on our other products and services or to obtain technical support, please contact our Customer Care Department within the United States at (866) 744-2665, or outside the United States at (510) 253-0500.

Rockridge Press publishes its books in a variety of electronic and print formats. Some content that appears in print may not be available in electronic books, and vice versa.

Interior and Cover Designer: Joshua Moore
Photo Art Director: Karen Beard
Editor: Jeanine Le Ny
Production Editor: Andrew Yackira
Photography: © 2018 Marija Vidal. Author photo courtesy of Mindy Altman Photo.

ISBN: Print 978-1-64152-341-7 | eBook 978-1-64152-342-4

To Jace and Aria,
You're my inspiration in everything
I do. Love you to the moon and back.

● ● ● ●

CONTENTS

• • • •

INTRODUCTION

● ● ● ●

I'LL NEVER FORGET the day when my obsession with slime began. I was on my kitchen floor with my two kids, Jace and Aria. We were desperately trying to make slime for the first time. Even though it took 10 tries until we finally got it right, we had so much fun learning and experimenting. My kids and I love playing with the oozy, gooey, stretchy substance. It's like one big science experiment! We started off making basic recipes together, and then we tried more complicated ones. Before long, we were tinkering with our own slimy creations—because that's what good scientists do! Now our craft closet is overrun with tubs and tubs of awesome slime. We've learned a lot along the way, and I want to share it all with you!

Secrets of Slime Recipe Book will show you everything you need to know to make the best slime at home. This book isn't just about learning the coolest slime recipes; it's also about sharing the secrets that will help you develop your own unique creations. You'll learn what tools a savvy slimer needs to have on hand, what to do if your slime goes wrong, and the science behind slime itself. You'll get to try 30 recipes that range from basic slime to more advanced ones, such as the amazing Avalanche Slime (page 76). Once you're ready to get sliming on your own, Chapter 4 (page 81) will help you create your own original slime recipes. You will experiment with your own slime designs and record it all in the Slime Diary (page 87) at the end of the book.

So, gather your supplies, pick your workstation, and let's make some squishy, stretchy slime!

BE A SLIMER!

● ● ● ●

In this section, we go over the basics of what slime is and how to make it. By the end of the chapter, you'll be ready to start making your own slimes. Let's begin!

SLIME HISTORY

It all started in 1976, when slime was first created and sold by the toy company Mattel. Once people realized how easy it was to make slime at home, they started to create their own. Recently, making and playing with it has become a worldwide phenomenon that you've probably seen all over social media. Luckily for us, slime has gotten a lot more advanced since it was created, and now there are so many unique ways to make it.

The recipes in this book offer you many different ways to make and enhance your slime. We start with a simple saline-and-glue technique to make Basic Slime (page 11) in Chapter 2, and move all the way up to more advanced techniques, such as Chalkboard Slime (page 47) and Apple Pie Jelly Cube Slime (page 63). Before we start making it, though, let's go over the basics of slime.

SLIME BASICS

So, what exactly is this stretchy, sticky substance made of? Well, it all starts with glue. Glue is made up of polymers, which are strings of molecules bonded together. Slime is made when boron (your activator) mixes with the glue's polymer chains. This creates strong and flexible bonds between the molecules, giving the glue a thick, oozy texture. After you knead it, the mixture stops being sticky and starts turning into slime. Now that you know what slime is, I'll bet you want to know how to make it, right? It's simple! Here's an overview of what you'll need:

POLYVINYL ACETATE (PVA) GLUE: This is a basic nontoxic glue that comes in either white or clear. You can find it at any department store or craft store or online. It comes in small bottles and gallon jugs. I suggest buying the gallon jugs if you are going to make several batches of slime.

ACTIVATOR: The activator is the most important ingredient in a slime recipe. This is a liquid ingredient that binds your mixture together. Adding the correct amount of activator to the glue activates the polymer

molecules so that they become stretchy and form your slime. There are a few different activators that you can use, but we prefer the borax-powder-free method using saline solution. When mixing glue with saline solution, you have to make sure that the saline solution contains sodium borate and boric acid; otherwise, your slime will not form. You'll mix the saline solution with diluted baking soda to use as your slime activator before adding it to your glue mixture.

NO BORAX POWDER

Borax is an ingredient in many laundry and cleaning products. Many parents are hesitant to let their kids handle slimes made with borax powder after news reports of kids having bad skin reactions. The good news is that the slime recipes in this book do not contain any borax powder. I think borax-based slimes are harder to make anyway. Saline solution mixed with diluted baking soda is our choice as an activator. As I mentioned earlier, it's important to make sure the solution contains boric acid and sodium borate. Although these ingredients are similar to borax, saline solution contains a very small amount of them, and it is safer to use than borax powder.

ADD-INS: You can create super-colorful and textured slime by adding ingredients such as:

- Glitter
- Craft foam beads
- Food coloring
- Pigment
- Acrylic paint
- Instant snow
- Crayola Model Magic clay

- Fishbowl beads
- Water beads
- Phosphorescent powder
- Kinetic sand
- Shaving cream
- Magic Eraser sponge
- And more!

DON'T EAT THE SLIME AND OTHER SAFETY NOTES

Since you will be conducting science experiments, it's important to make sure we use basic safety precautions. Here's a quick checklist of some dos and don'ts for all things slime.

DO:

- **ASK** an adult for permission before making slime, and it's important for them to supervise and help you.

- **WEAR** plastic gloves while handling slime ingredients if you have sensitive skin. If you notice any skin irritation, stop making or playing with slime immediately.

- **BE** exact with measurements. Slime recipes involve chemical reactions, with specific ingredients chosen to activate the reaction.

- **WASH** your hands thoroughly with soap and water after handling slime.

- **DISINFECT** your slime area and tools when you're finished making slime.

DON'T:

- **MIX** activators. Use only one type of activator for each batch of slime.

- **RUB** your eyes until after you've properly washed your hands.

- **EAT** slime, and never put any of the slime ingredients in your mouth. While two of the slimes are labeled as taste-safe, you should taste only a tiny amount.

- **STORE** your slime where small children or pets can get to it.

- **MAKE** slime near a carpet. It's very hard to clean up.

GEAR UP!

Here's a list of the things you'll need to get started. These tools should be used for slime making only; store them away from the kitchen so that they are not used for cooking.

- **BOWLS WITH LIDS:** You'll need medium and large mixing bowls with lids.

- **MEASURING SPOONS AND CUPS:** You'll need measuring spoons to measure dry ingredients and a measuring cup to measure liquids.

- **MIXING UTENSILS:** You can use anything you want, including spoons, spatulas, and even large disposable craft sticks. Just make sure that you use them only for slime making, and don't use utensils from your kitchen.

- **AIRTIGHT CONTAINERS:** Slime can last for weeks or months depending on your ingredients and whether it's stored properly. Put your slimes in airtight containers when you've finished playing with them so you can play with them again later.

SLIME SECRET: TIPS FOR IN THE LAB

You'll need a clean area where all the magic will take place. Pick a surface that isn't carpeted—slime is a nightmare to get out of carpeting. I make slime either outside or on the kitchen floor. Regardless of where I'm working, I always stock up on inexpensive shower curtains to lay down as my work space. They protect floors and make cleaning up really easy. When you're finished making slime, just pick up the shower curtain and toss it in the trash! It's also a good idea to wear old clothes or an apron while making slime. Tie your hair back if it's long, because the process can be a little messy. Clearly label all of your slime ingredients, and store them in bins to keep them organized. Label the bins too so that they are easily recognizable.

BECOME A SLIME SCIENTIST

As you progress through the book, you'll start to understand slime and what it does. All of the slime recipes include step-by-step instructions and color photos. The book starts out with easier slimes with Slime Apprentice: Starter Slimes (page 9). These are the slime recipes that you'll want to master first. Then you can advance to Super Slimer: Next-Level Slimes (page 43), which has intermediate slimes such as Magnetic Slime Machine and Avalanche Slime. The last chapter, Slime Scientist: Your Very Own Slimes (page 81), is all about making your very own slimes.

Keep an eye out for my Step It Up ideas to help you take your slimes to the next level. At the end of the book, you'll find a Slime Diary (page 87) where you can record your creations and results from your slime-making adventures. There are also science facts and slime tips throughout the book, so you will have all the information you need to become a successful slimer!

CHAPTER 2

SLIME APPRENTICE: STARTER SLIMES

• • • •

Want to be a super slimer? It's not so hard. Just follow the instructions for these 15 starter slimes, and you'll see how simple it is! My personal favorites are Fluffy Slime and Holographic Slime. How about you? Once you've mastered the basics, you can experiment to make the recipes yours. I've given you some extra ideas to get you started, but don't be afraid to try your own! Happy sliming!

BASIC SLIME

●●●●

Learn how to make your own homemade slime with this simple recipe using saline solution! The first time I made slime with my kids, we failed a few times before we got the mixture right. Our problem was caused by not kneading the slime enough and adding in too much activator. This basic recipe is the main building block for the slimes in the rest of the book. Don't worry if you don't get it right the first time. Go back, check your measurements, and try again! Then try making the slime a few more times to perfect it before moving on. Once you master Basic Slime, you'll be able to grow your slime knowledge in no time.

MATERIALS:

½ cup hot tap water

½ teaspoon baking soda

½ cup white PVA glue
  (or clear PVA glue)

2 to 3 tablespoons saline
  solution containing
  sodium borate
  and boric acid

Measuring cup

Measuring spoons

3 medium bowls

Mixing tools (spoons, craft
  sticks, or a spatula)

WHAT YOU DO:

1. Combine the hot tap water and baking soda in a medium bowl and stir until the baking soda is completely dissolved.

2. Next add the white (or clear) PVA glue and mix well. ➡

3. Now put in the saline solution a little at a time. Start by adding ½ tablespoon and stirring. Repeat until the mixture starts to clump up.

4. Mix until your slime begins taking on a ball-like form. It will begin coming off the sides of your bowl and sticking together.

5. Start kneading the slime with your hands. It will be very sticky at first, but as you continue to knead it, the slime will become less sticky and more solid. If it remains very sticky after kneading it a while, add in 1 teaspoon of saline solution at a time until you get your desired consistency. However, don't overdo it. Too much activator can make your slime tough and not stretchy.

STEP IT UP: Give your basic slime some color by adding 2 to 3 drops of food coloring after you mix in your PVA glue.

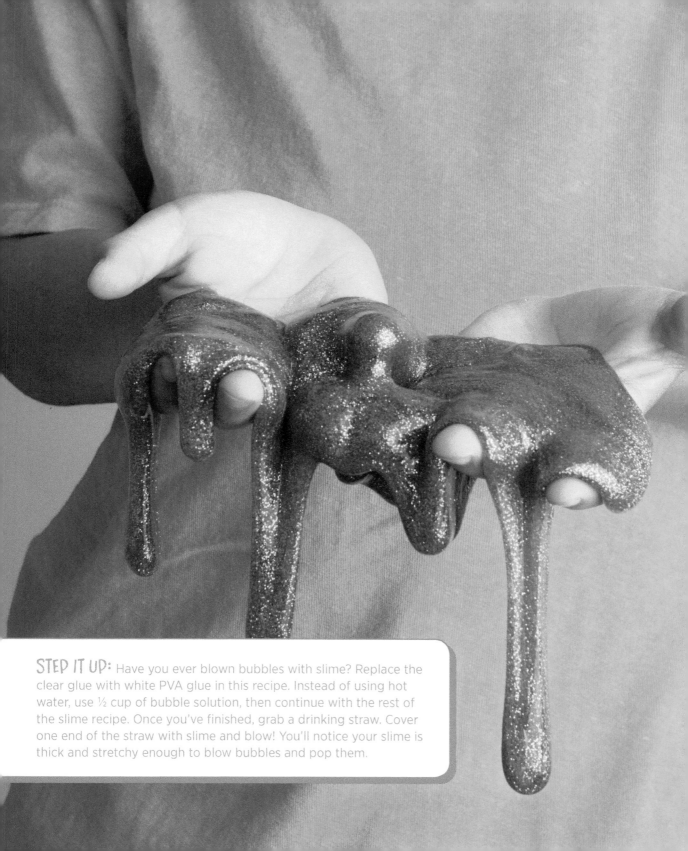

STEP IT UP: Have you ever blown bubbles with slime? Replace the clear glue with white PVA glue in this recipe. Instead of using hot water, use ½ cup of bubble solution, then continue with the rest of the slime recipe. Once you've finished, grab a drinking straw. Cover one end of the straw with slime and blow! You'll notice your slime is thick and stretchy enough to blow bubbles and pop them.

GLITTER BOMB SLIME

●●●●

Everything's better with glitter, especially slime! You can make Glitter Bomb Slime using glitter glue, but I prefer adding my own glitter to regular glue. This way I can choose the amount of glitter I want and its texture. Plus I get to have lots of fun with sparkly add-ins.

MATERIALS:

½ cup hot tap water

½ teaspoon baking soda

½ cup clear PVA glue

3 drops purple food coloring (optional)

1 to 2 tablespoons purple glitter

2 to 3 tablespoons saline solution containing sodium borate and boric acid

Measuring cup

Measuring spoons

Medium bowl

Mixing tools (spoons, craft sticks, or a spatula)

WHAT YOU DO:

1. Combine the hot tap water and baking soda in a medium bowl and stir until the baking soda is completely dissolved.

2. Next add the clear PVA glue and mix well. Then add the purple food coloring (if using).

3. Now it's time to mix in purple glitter! Use 1 to 2 tablespoons.

4. Next, put in the saline solution a little at a time. Start by adding ½ tablespoon and stirring. Repeat until the mixture starts to clump up.

5. Mix until your slime begins taking on a ball-like form. It will begin coming off the sides of your bowl and sticking together.

6. Start kneading the slime with your hands. It will be very sticky at first, but as you continue to knead it, the slime will become less sticky and more solid. If it remains very sticky after kneading it a while, add in a teaspoon of saline solution at a time until you get your desired consistency. However, don't overdo it. Too much activator can make your slime tough and not stretchy.

FLUFFY SLIME

● ● ● ●

Now that you've got the basic slime recipe down, you can start experimenting with texture. This recipe will give you a soft, stretchy, and fun fluffy slime. This recipe takes only minutes but will entertain you for hours!

MATERIALS:

½ cup white PVA glue

2 cups shaving cream

3 drops orange food coloring (optional)

¼ teaspoon baking soda

1 tablespoon saline solution containing sodium borate and boric acid

Measuring cup

Measuring spoons

Large bowl

Mixing tools (spoons, craft sticks, or a spatula)

WHAT YOU DO:

1. Mix the white PVA glue and the shaving cream in a large bowl.

2. Add the orange food coloring (if using). Then stir in the baking soda.

3. Now, put in the saline solution a little at a time. Start by adding ½ tablespoon and stirring. Repeat until the mixture starts to clump up.

4. Mix until your slime begins taking on a ball-like form. It will begin coming off the sides of your bowl and sticking together.

5. Start kneading the slime with your hands. It will be very sticky at first, but as you continue to knead it, the slime will become less sticky and more solid. If it remains very sticky after kneading it a while, add in a teaspoon of saline solution at a time until you get your desired consistency. However, don't overdo it. Too much activator can make your slime tough and not stretchy.

STEP IT UP: Add in a few drops of your favorite scented oil after step 2 to make the slime smell good. Use only a tiny amount—1 or 2 drops—because a little goes a long way.

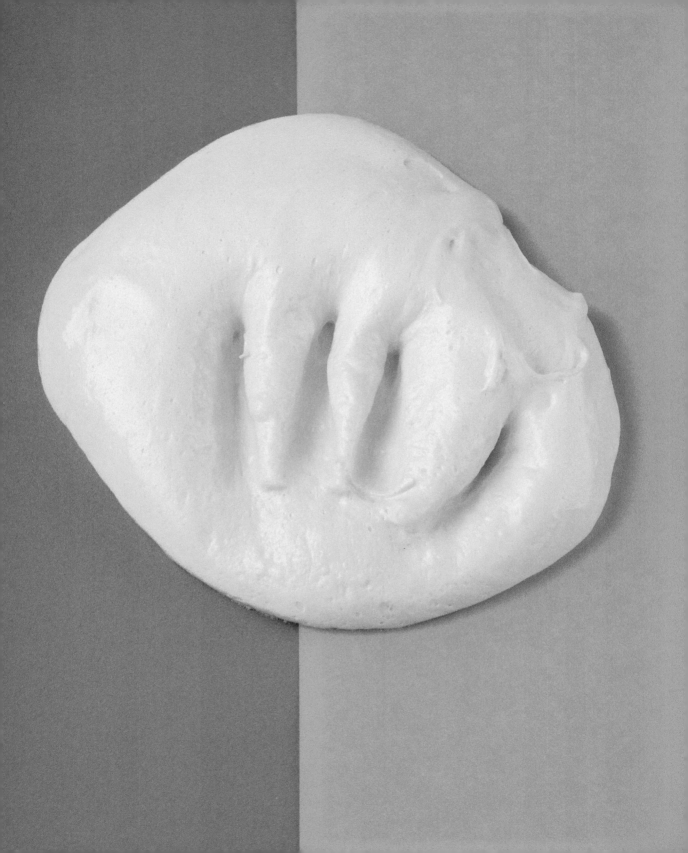

FLOAM SLIME

● ● ● ●

Floam is a slime-like substance that contains small polystyrene foam beads, and it can hold its shape when you press your hand or fingers into it. It also makes a cool sound when you play with it. I love hearing that popping noise when I squeeze this slime through my fingers.

MATERIALS:

½ **cup hot tap water**

½ **teaspoon baking soda**

½ **cup white PVA glue**

½ **to 1 cup polystyrene foam beads**

2 to 3 tablespoons saline solution containing sodium borate and boric acid

Measuring cup

Measuring spoons

Medium bowl

Mixing tools (spoons, craft sticks, or a spatula)

SLIME SECRET:

Experiment with your floam's texture with different amounts of foam beads. Lots of beads will make your slime crunchy and moldable. Adding a small amount will keep it super stretchy.

WHAT YOU DO:

1. Combine the hot tap water and baking soda in a bowl and stir until the baking soda is completely dissolved.

2. Add the white PVA glue and mix well.

3. Now it's time to mix in the polystyrene foam beads. Start with ½ cup and stir well to incorporate. Add more foam beads depending on the consistency you want.

4. Next, put in the saline solution a little at a time. Start by adding ½ tablespoon and stirring. Repeat until the mixture starts to clump up.

5. Mix until your slime begins taking on a ball-like form. It will begin coming off the sides of your bowl and sticking together.

6. Start kneading the slime with your hands. It will be very sticky at first, but as you continue to knead it, the slime will become less sticky and more solid. If it remains very sticky after kneading it a while, add in a teaspoon of saline solution at a time until you get your desired consistency. However, don't overdo it. Too much activator can make your slime tough and not stretchy.

TOXIC WASTE SLIME

● ● ● ●

Want to find out how to make stretchy slime glow? The secret to the best glow-in-the-dark slime is to use phosphorescent powder. There are glow-in-the-dark glues that you can use as well, but we've found that using the powder creates a brighter glowing effect.

MATERIALS:

½ cup hot tap water

½ teaspoon baking soda

½ cup clear PVA glue

½ tablespoon glow powder

2 to 3 tablespoons saline
   solution containing
   sodium borate
   and boric acid

Measuring cup

Measuring spoons

Medium bowl

Mixing tools (spoons, craft
   sticks, or a spatula)

Light source, such
   as a lamp

SLIME SCIENCE: So, how does Toxic Waste Slime work? The phosphorescent powder inside absorbs some of the light's energy. Once you remove the light source, the powder slowly releases the stored energy, which you see when it glows.

WHAT YOU DO:

1. Combine the hot tap water and baking soda in a bowl and stir until the baking soda is completely dissolved.

2. Next add the clear PVA glue and mix well.

3. Then mix in the glow powder.

4. Now, put in the saline solution a little at a time. Start by adding ½ tablespoon and stirring. Repeat until the mixture starts to clump up.

5. Mix until your slime begins taking on a ball-like form. It will begin coming off the sides of your bowl and sticking together.

6. Start kneading the slime with your hands. It will be very sticky at first, but as you continue to knead it, the slime will become less sticky and more solid. If it remains very sticky after kneading it a while, add in a teaspoon of saline solution at a time until you get your desired consistency. However, don't overdo it. Too much activator can make your slime tough and not stretchy.

7. "Charge" your slime by setting it under a light source for a few minutes. Then take it to a dark place and watch it glow!

BUTTER SLIME

This slime isn't actually made with butter, but it looks and feels like it is! It has a soft texture that is not as stretchy as some of the other slimes in this book. Instead, it's moldable and fluffy.

MATERIALS:

½ cup hot tap water

½ teaspoon baking soda

½ cup white PVA glue

2 to 3 tablespoons saline solution containing sodium borate and boric acid

3 ounces red Crayola Model Magic air-dry clay

Measuring cup

Measuring spoons

Medium bowl

Mixing tools (spoons, craft sticks, or a spatula)

WHAT YOU DO:

1. Combine the hot tap water and baking soda in a bowl and stir until the baking soda is completely dissolved.

2. Next add the white PVA glue and mix well.

3. Now, put in the saline solution a little at a time. Start by adding ½ tablespoon and stirring. Repeat until the mixture starts to clump up.

4. Mix until your slime begins taking on a ball-like form. It will begin coming off the sides of your bowl and sticking together.

5. Start kneading the slime with your hands. It will be very sticky at first, but as you continue to knead it, the slime will become less sticky and more solid. If it remains very sticky after kneading it a while, add in a teaspoon of saline solution at a time until you get your desired consistency. However, don't overdo it. Too much activator can make your slime tough and not stretchy.

6. Add the Crayola Model Magic air-dry clay into your slime. Knead and pull until it's thoroughly mixed in with your slime. This will take a few minutes.

SLIME SECRET: Butter Slime is always stretchy when you first make it. But it might get hard if it sits out, unused, for an hour or more. Make sure to seal the slime in an airtight container when you are finished playing with it.

STEP IT UP: Experiment with different amounts of instant snow to make a thicker cloud-like slime. Because of the water used to activate the instant snow, you may notice your slime getting stickier when you add in more of it. If that's the case, simply add in more activator, ½ tablespoon at a time, until you get your desired consistency.

CLOUD NINE SLIME

●●●●

Cloud slime is fluffy and looks just like a cloud. You can add any color you'd like to this slime or keep it white to look like a real cloud. The secret to making Cloud Nine Slime is using instant snow! It comes in a tiny package and expands when you add water. Making slime with instant snow can be a little tricky, but the key is to add in small amounts of instant snow powder at a time.

MATERIALS:

½ **cup hot tap water**

½ **teaspoon baking soda**

½ **cup white PVA glue**

3 drops green food coloring (optional)

2 to 3 tablespoons saline solution containing sodium borate and boric acid

½ **cup instant snow, made according to package instructions**

Measuring cup

Measuring spoons

Medium bowl

Mixing tools (spoons, craft sticks, or a spatula)

WHAT YOU DO:

1. Combine the hot tap water and baking soda in a bowl and stir until the baking soda is completely dissolved.

2. Next add the white PVA glue and mix thoroughly.

3. Then mix in the green food coloring (if using).

4. Now, put in the saline solution a little at a time. Start by adding ½ tablespoon and then stirring. Repeat until the mixture starts to clump up.

5. Mix until your slime begins taking on a ball-like form. It will begin coming off the sides of your bowl and sticking together.

6. Start kneading the slime with your hands. It will be very sticky at first, but as you continue to knead it, the slime will become less sticky and more solid. If it remains very sticky after kneading it a while, add in a teaspoon of saline solution at a time until you get your desired consistency. However, don't overdo it. Too much activator can make your slime tough and not stretchy.

7. Add the instant snow to your slime. Mix and enjoy!

CRUNCHY FISHBOWL SLIME

• • • •

Crunchy Fishbowl Slime has an awesome texture. Twist and squeeze this slime, and you will hear fun popping sounds!

MATERIALS:

½ cup hot tap water

½ teaspoon baking soda

½ cup clear PVA glue

3 drops blue food coloring (optional)

2 to 3 tablespoons saline solution containing sodium borate and boric acid

1 cup transparent fishbowl filler beads

Measuring cup

Measuring spoons

Medium bowl

Mixing tools (spoons, craft sticks, or a spatula)

SLIME SECRET: Be careful not to add too many fishbowl beads or your slime may lose its stretch.

WHAT YOU DO:

1. Combine the hot tap water and baking soda in a bowl and stir until the baking soda is completely dissolved.

2. Next add the clear PVA glue and mix well.

3. Then mix in the blue food coloring (if using).

4. Now, put in the saline solution a little at a time. Start by adding ½ tablespoon and stirring. Repeat until the mixture starts to clump up.

5. Mix until your slime begins taking on a ball-like form. It will begin coming off the sides of your bowl and sticking together.

6. Start kneading the slime with your hands. It will be very sticky at first, but as you knead it, the slime will become less sticky and more solid. If it remains very sticky after kneading it a while, add in a teaspoon of saline solution at a time until you get your desired consistency. However, don't overdo it. Too much activator can make your slime tough and not stretchy. It's okay if the slime is a bit sticky; it'll make it easier for the fishbowl beads to stick.

7. Knead ½ cup of fishbowl filler beads into the slime. If you want to add more beads, keep in mind that the more beads you add, the crunchier your slime will be.

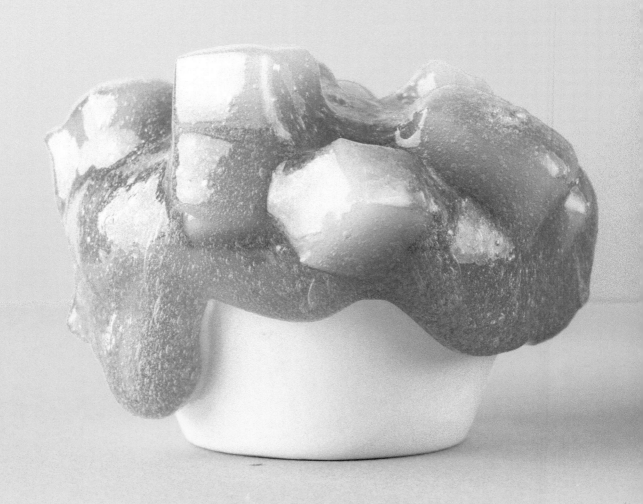

JELLY CUBE SLIME

● ● ● ●

Jelly Cube Slime is fun to play with because of the Magic Eraser sponge cubes inside. After you make this slime, squeeze the sponges with your fingers to create a satisfying slushy texture.

MATERIALS:

1 Magic Eraser sponge

½ cup hot tap water

½ teaspoon baking soda

3 drops purple food coloring (optional)

2 to 3 tablespoons saline solution containing sodium borate and boric acid

Scissors

Measuring cup

Measuring spoons

Medium bowl

Mixing tools (spoons, craft sticks, or a spatula)

SLIME SECRET: Add the Magic Eraser cubes while the slime is sticky so the pieces don't fall out. You might need to use more activator than usual.

WHAT YOU DO:

1. Using scissors, cut your Magic Eraser sponge into small cubes and set aside.

2. Combine the hot tap water and baking soda in a bowl and stir until the baking soda is completely dissolved.

3. Next mix the clear PVA glue and mix well.

4. Then add in the purple food coloring (if using).

5. Now, put in the saline solution a little at a time. Start by adding ½ tablespoon and stirring. Repeat until the mixture starts to clump up.

6. Mix until your slime begins taking on a ball-like form. It will begin coming off the sides of your bowl and sticking together.

7. Add the cubes of Magic Eraser sponge to the mixture.

8. Start kneading the slime with your hands. It will be very sticky at first but, as you continue to knead it, the slime will become less sticky and more solid. If it remains very sticky after kneading it a while, add in a teaspoon of saline solution at a time until you get your desired consistency. However, don't overdo it. Too much activator can make your slime tough and not stretchy.

PIRATE'S TREASURE SLIME

● ● ● ●

This slime is mesmerizing and fun to play with. The best part: It's super easy to make! My kids love twisting and stretching this slime. The chunky gold coins swirled in with the metallic gold color gives it the perfect pirate treasure look.

MATERIALS:

½ **cup hot tap water**

½ **teaspoon baking soda**

½ **cup clear PVA glue**

1 **tablespoon gold glitter (optional)**

2 **to 3 tablespoons saline solution containing sodium borate and boric acid**

1 **teaspoon metallic gold pigment powder**

Gold-colored coins

Measuring cup

Measuring spoons

Medium bowl

Mixing tools (spoons, craft sticks, or a spatula)

SLIME SECRET: Using pigment powder gives your slime a much more vibrant look than if you use metallic paint.

WHAT YOU DO:

1. Combine the hot tap water and baking soda in a bowl and stir until it's completely dissolved.

2. Next add the clear PVA glue and mix well.

3. Then add in the gold glitter (if using), and mix well.

4. Now, put in the saline solution a little at a time. Start by adding ½ tablespoon and stirring. Repeat until the mixture starts to clump up.

5. Mix until your slime begins taking on a ball-like form. It will begin coming off the sides of your bowl and sticking together.

6. Start kneading the slime with your hands. It will be very sticky at first but, as you continue to knead it, the slime will become less sticky and more solid. If it remains very sticky after kneading it a while, add in a teaspoon of saline solution at a time until you get your desired consistency. However, don't overdo it. Too much activator can make your slime tough and not stretchy.

7. Next use your finger and form a small indentation in the middle of your slime, and pour the metallic gold pigment powder into it. Fold the edges of your slime into the middle so that you can fold and knead the pigment powder into the slime. Add a few gold-colored coins and fold them in.

ALL-NATURAL TASTE-SAFE SLIME

● ● ● ●

This recipe is one of the easiest taste-safe recipes out there. We will be using a fiber supplement as the main ingredient. For this recipe to work, you must choose a fiber supplement that has psyllium listed as the active ingredient. Also, ask an adult to help you with this slime, since you will be cooking it!

MATERIALS:

3 cups water

3 tablespoons organic whole-husk psyllium fiber supplement

Large pot

WHAT YOU DO:

1. Bring the water to a boil.
2. Add the organic whole-husk psyllium to the boiling water.
3. Lower to medium heat.
4. Stir for a few minutes. You'll notice the psyllium will start to thicken into a gel.
5. Remove from the heat and set aside to cool down. The psyllium will start to turn an orange color. Once it's completely cooled down, you can play!

STEP IT UP: You can add your favorite Kool-Aid powder to change the color. After you add the psyllium in step 2, add a 0.13-ounce packet of Kool-Aid. Your slime will still be taste-safe, and it will smell good, too.

HOLOGRAPHIC SLIME

● ● ● ●

This Holographic Slime is out-of-this-world mesmerizing. It creates shimmery rainbow colors that reflect in different lighting. I use a basic clear saline solution recipe that is mixed with a holographic pigment powder. You can find holographic pigment at a beauty supply store or online. Shine a light on your slime or take it outside, and you'll be hypnotized by the three-dimensional rainbows!

MATERIALS:

½ cup hot tap water

½ teaspoon baking soda

½ cup clear PVA glue

2 to 3 tablespoons saline solution containing sodium borate and boric acid

¼ to ½ teaspoon holographic pigment powder

Measuring cup

Measuring spoons

Medium bowl

Mixing tools (spoons, craft sticks, or a spatula)

STEP IT UP: If you want to make this holographic slime even more mesmerizing, add an equal amount of holographic glitter when you are folding in the pigment powder.

WHAT YOU DO:

1. Combine the hot tap water and baking soda in a bowl and stir until the baking soda is completely dissolved.

2. Next add the clear PVA glue and mix well.

3. Now, put in the saline solution a little at a time. Start by adding ½ tablespoon and stirring. Repeat until the mixture starts to clump up.

4. Mix until your slime begins taking on a ball-like form. It will begin coming off the sides of your bowl and sticking together.

5. Start kneading the slime with your hands. It will be very sticky at first, but as you continue to knead it, the slime will become less sticky and more solid. If it remains very sticky after kneading it a while, add in a teaspoon of saline solution at a time until you get your desired consistency. However, don't overdo it. Too much activator can make your slime tough and not stretchy.

6. Next, form a small indentation in the middle of your slime, and add ¼ teaspoon of the holographic pigment powder to it. Fold over your slime to mix in your pigment. If you think your slime needs more, add the rest and knead.

TASTE-SAFE MARSHMALLOW FLUFF SLIME

● ● ● ●

Did you know that there are ingredients right in your kitchen that are perfect for making slime? This Taste-Safe Marshmallow Fluff Slime is stretchy, and it's simple because it is made with only two ingredients. A lot of taste–safe slimes have a Play-Doh-like texture, but this marshmallow fluff still has a lot of stretch to it! Taste away, but don't eat a significant amount.

MATERIALS:

½ **cup powdered sugar, plus more as needed**

½ **cup marshmallow fluff**

WHAT YOU DO:

1. Pour the powdered sugar onto a clean, smooth surface and then spoon your marshmallow fluff on top.
2. Knead the powdered sugar into the marshmallow fluff until you get your desired consistency.
3. If it's still sticky, knead in more powdered sugar until it's no longer sticky.
4. Under an adult's supervision, take a small taste of the slime. What do you think?

SLIME SECRET: If you don't have any marshmallow fluff on hand, you can use ½ cup of store-bought frosting instead.

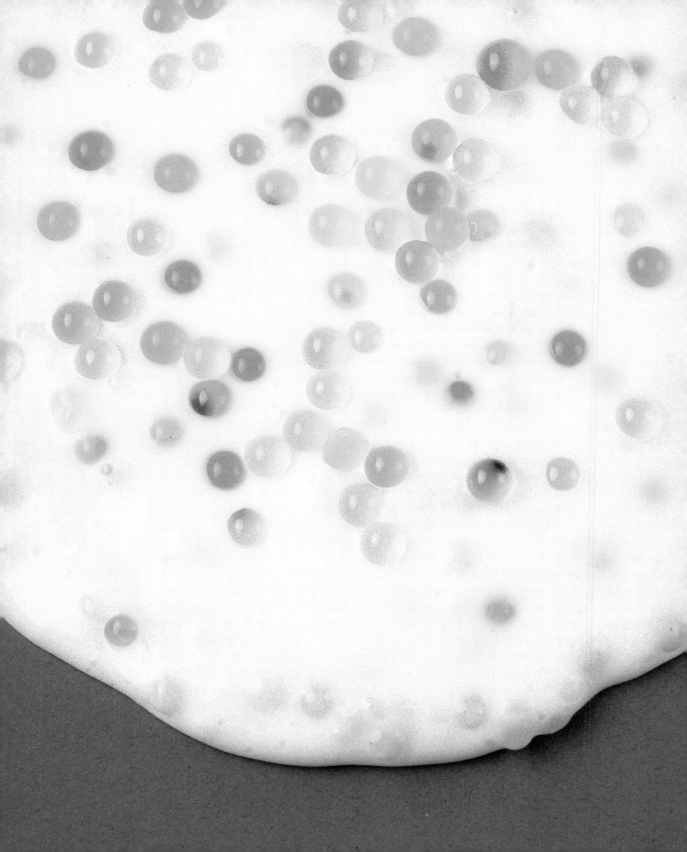

GOOEY WATER BEAD SLIME

●●●●

My daughter has a foot spa where you dip your feet into a tub filled with squishy water beads. Because the spa is so relaxing, I thought it might be even more relaxing—and fun—to play with water beads in slime. Guess what? It is!

MATERIALS:

½ cup water beads

½ cup hot water

½ teaspoon baking soda

½ cup white PVA glue

2 to 3 tablespoons saline solution containing sodium borate and boric acid

Measuring cup

Measuring spoons

Medium bowl

Mixing tools (spoons, craft sticks, or a spatula)

SLIME SECRET: If you ever have a slime that you want to dispose of, add some flour to the mixture. This will dry it out so that it's easier to throw away.

WHAT YOU DO:

1. Start by hydrating the water beads following the directions on the package. Set aside.

2. Combine the hot tap water and baking soda in a bowl and stir until the baking soda is completely dissolved.

3. Next add the white PVA glue and mix well.

4. Now, put in the saline solution a little at a time. Start by adding ½ tablespoon and stirring. Repeat until the mixture starts to clump up.

5. Mix until your slime begins taking on a ball-like form. It will begin coming off the sides of your bowl and sticking together.

6. Add the water beads.

7. Start kneading the slime with your hands. It will be very sticky at first, but as you continue to knead it, the slime will become less sticky and more solid. If it remains very sticky after kneading it a while, add in a teaspoon of saline solution at a time until you get your desired consistency. However, don't overdo it. Too much activator can make your slime tough and not stretchy.

GROOVY TIE-DYE SLIME

● ● ● ●

Groovy Tie-Dye Slime is so bright and stretchy! You'll use neon acrylic paint in this recipe. It's a lot brighter than neon food coloring. When you pull and mix the fun colors, it looks just like a tie-dye design in your slime.

MATERIALS:

1½ cups hot tap water

1½ teaspoons baking soda

1½ cups white PVA glue

3 to 4 drops neon pink acrylic paint

3 to 4 drops neon green acrylic paint

3 to 4 drops neon yellow acrylic paint

6 to 9 tablespoons saline solution containing sodium borate and boric acid

Measuring cup

Measuring spoons

Large bowl

3 medium bowls

Mixing tools (spoons, craft sticks, or a spatula)

STEP IT UP: Mix in 1½ cups of shaving cream along with your glue in step 2 for a fluffy version of this slime. It will feel fluffy while still looking far out.

WHAT YOU DO:

1. Combine the hot tap water and baking soda in a large bowl and stir until the baking soda is completely dissolved.

2. Next add the white PVA glue and mix well.

3. Evenly divide the mixture into 3 bowls. Add neon pink paint to one, neon green paint to the second, and add neon yellow paint to the last. Mix each thoroughly.

4. In the first bowl, begin stirring in the saline solution ½ tablespoon at a time. Repeat until the mixture starts to clump up. I normally use between 2 and 3 tablespoons of saline solution.

5. Mix until your slime begins taking on a ball-like form. It will begin coming off the sides of your bowl and sticking together.

6. Start kneading the slime with your hands. It will be very sticky at first, but as you continue to knead it, the slime will become more solid. If it remains very sticky after kneading it a while, add in a teaspoon of saline solution at a time until you get your desired consistency.

7. Repeat steps 4 through 6 for the other two slimes. Be sure to wash your hands after kneading each one so that you don't mix colors.

8. Lay each slime side by side on a flat, protected surface. Twist and pull the colors to create a true tie-dye look.

SUPER SLIMER:
NEXT-LEVEL SLIMES

● ● ● ●

Now that you've mastered the basics, you can venture on to the more challenging slimes. In this chapter we will build upon the slimes that you made earlier in the book, and with patience and practice you'll be making them like a master slimer in no time. Come on, let's slime!

TASTE-SAFE GUMMY BEAR SLIME

● ● ● ●

This edible gummy bear slime can be made in just a few minutes. It has a marshmallow-like consistency like our edible Taste-Safe Marshmallow Fluff Slime (page 36), and it smells amazing! This recipe is great to play with right after you make it, but I wouldn't recommend storing it for play later because it will get hard quickly. You can use gummy bears that are all the same color or a mixture, whichever you prefer.

MATERIALS:

2 cups gummy bears

4 tablespoons
    powdered sugar

4 tablespoons cornstarch

Measuring cup

Measuring spoons

Medium bowl

Mixing tools (spoons, craft
    sticks, or a spatula)

WHAT YOU DO:

1. Heat the gummy bears in the microwave for 10 seconds and stir. Keep heating the gummy bears for 10 seconds and mixing until they are melted down completely.

2. Once the liquid has cooled slightly (ask an adult to tell you when it is safe enough to handle), knead in the powdered sugar and cornstarch in equal amounts until your mixture forms a slime-like consistency. Sprinkle any extra gummy bears on top, for decoration.

STEP IT UP: Try other candies like Starburst or Laffy Taffy to see how your slime varies in consistency.

CHALKBOARD SLIME

We're combining chemistry and art with this hands-on recipe. This slime is black, and you can doodle on it with chalk markers. Stretch and pull your slime to change the look of your designs. Then knead your slime to start over again with a blank canvas!

MATERIALS:

½ cup white PVA glue

3 tablespoons chalkboard paint

1 teaspoon baking soda

2 to 3 tablespoons saline solution containing sodium borate and boric acid

Chalk markers

Measuring cup

Measuring spoons

Medium bowl

Mixing tools (spoons, craft sticks, or a spatula)

Rolling pin

SLIME SECRET: Don't draw on your slime like you would with paper because the tip of your marker will get stuck. Doodle on the slime by pressing lightly with a dabbing motion.

WHAT YOU DO:

1. Combine the white PVA glue and the chalkboard paint in a bowl. Mix thoroughly.

2. Next mix in the baking soda.

3. Now, put in the saline solution a little at a time. Start by adding ½ tablespoon and stirring. Repeat until the mixture starts to clump up.

4. Mix until your slime begins taking on a ball-like form. It will begin coming off the sides of your bowl and sticking together.

5. Start kneading the slime with your hands. It will be very sticky at first, but as you continue to knead it, the slime will become less sticky and more solid. If it remains very sticky after kneading it a while, add in a teaspoon of saline solution at a time until you get your desired consistency. However, don't overdo it. Too much activator can make your slime tough and not stretchy.

6. Put your slime on a flat, protected surface and use a rolling pin to flatten it out. Draw on your slime with the chalk markers. Then stretch and twist the patterns in your slime and watch them transform into new art.

7. Want to start over? Simply knead your slime, and your doodles will disappear. Roll it out and start drawing all over again.

COLOR-CHANGING SLIME

• • • •

Take your slime to the next level with this color-changing recipe using a thermochromic pigment! This slime will change colors depending on its temperature. Thermochromic pigments are available in a wide variety of colors and can be found easily online.

MATERIALS:

½ cup white PVA glue

½ teaspoon thermochromic pigment

½ tablespoon baking soda

2 to 3 tablespoons saline solution containing sodium borate and boric acid

Measuring cup

Measuring spoons

Medium bowl

Mixing tools (spoons, craft sticks, or a spatula)

WHAT YOU DO:

1. Combine the white PVA glue and thermochromic pigment in a bowl. Mix thoroughly until you see no dry spots.

2. Next mix in the baking soda.

3. Now, put in the saline solution a little at a time. Start by adding ½ tablespoon and then stirring. Repeat until the mixture starts to clump up.

4. Mix until your slime begins taking on a ball-like form. It will begin coming off the sides of your bowl and sticking together.

5. Start kneading the slime with your hands. It will be very sticky at first, but as you continue to knead it, the slime will become less sticky and more solid. If it remains very sticky after kneading it a while, add in a teaspoon of saline solution at a time until you get your desired consistency. However, don't overdo it. Too much activator can make your slime tough and not stretchy.

SLIME SCIENCE: To get the awesome contrasting colors, experiment with things that will change the slime's temperature. Press a warm hand into the slime. What happens when you pull it out? Now put an ice pack or a hand warmer on the slime. Record the results.

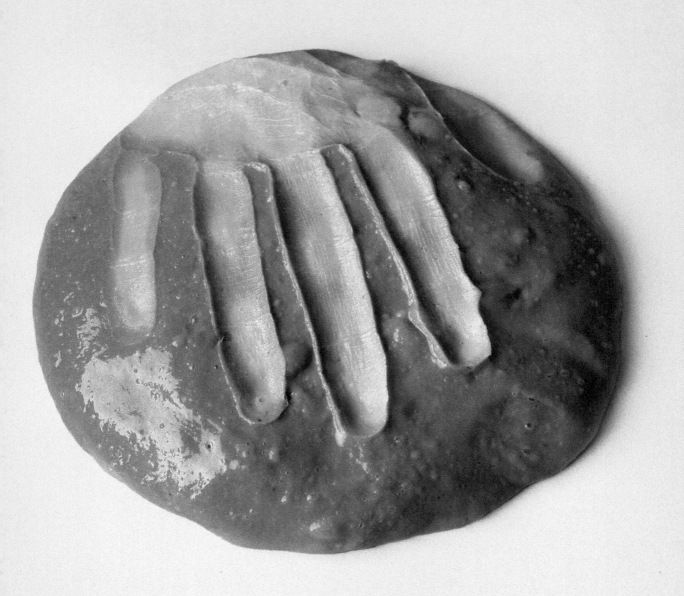

MAGNETIC SLIME MACHINE

Magnetic Slime Machine uses a supercool ingredient: magnetic powder! Set a magnet on top of the slime and watch it get swallowed up, or place it nearby and see the slime crawl toward the magnet. Magnetic powder is not safe to inhale or ingest, so be sure to wash your hands once you're finished.

MATERIALS:

½ cup hot tap water

½ teaspoon baking soda

½ cup white PVA glue

2 to 3 tablespoons saline solution containing sodium borate and boric acid

2 tablespoons iron oxide powder

Neodymium magnet (An ordinary magnet will not work.)

Measuring cup

Measuring spoons

Medium bowl

Mixing tools (spoons, craft sticks, or a spatula)

SLIME SCIENCE:

The iron oxide powder contains iron fillings, which are magnetic. The iron filings stay in the slime because of the force of two substances sticking together, resulting in magnetic slime.

WHAT YOU DO:

1. Combine the hot tap water and baking soda in a bowl and stir until the baking soda is completely dissolved.

2. Next add the clear PVA glue and mix well.

3. Now, put in the saline solution a little at a time. Start by adding ½ tablespoon and stirring. Repeat until the mixture starts to clump up.

4. Mix until your slime begins taking on a ball-like form. It will begin coming off the sides of your bowl and sticking together.

5. Start kneading the slime with your hands. It will be very sticky at first, but as you continue to knead it, the slime will become less sticky and more solid. If it remains sticky after kneading it a while, add in a teaspoon of saline solution at a time until you get your desired consistency.

6. Next use your finger to form a small indentation in the middle of your slime and pour in ½ tablespoon of iron oxide powder. Fold the edges of your slime into the middle so that you can mix the powder into the slime. Repeat the process of adding in ½ tablespoon of iron oxide powder and kneading until the slime reacts to the neodymium magnet. It should happen after adding around 2 tablespoons of the powder.

SLIME SECRET: The secret to making ocean slime is using clear glue as your base. If you use white glue, the color won't look like clear blue ocean water.

UNDER THE SEA SLIME

● ● ● ●

The great thing about slime is that you can customize it in so many ways. This recipe was inspired by my family's summer trip to the Outer Banks of North Carolina. We came back with a bucket full of seashells. One night we made a clear glittery blue slime, and the kids added in little seashells and toy ocean animals.

MATERIALS:

½ cup hot tap water

½ teaspoon baking soda

½ cup clear PVA glue

4 to 5 drops blue food coloring

1 to 2 tablespoons blue glitter

2 to 3 tablespoons saline solution containing sodium borate and boric acid

Small plastic ocean toys

Seashells

Measuring cup

Measuring spoons

Medium bowl

Mixing tools (spoons, craft sticks, or a spatula)

WHAT YOU DO:

1. Combine the hot tap water and baking soda in a bowl and stir until the baking soda is completely dissolved.

2. Next add the clear PVA glue and mix well.

3. Mix in 4 to 5 drops of blue food coloring and 1 to 2 tablespoons of blue glitter.

4. Now, put in the saline solution a little at a time. Start by adding ½ tablespoon and stirring. Repeat until the mixture starts to clump up.

5. Mix until your slime begins taking on a ball-like form. It will begin coming off the sides of your bowl and sticking together.

6. Start kneading the slime with your hands. It will be very sticky at first, but as you continue to knead it, the slime will become less sticky and more solid. If it remains very sticky after kneading it a while, add in a teaspoon of saline solution at a time until you get your desired consistency. However, don't overdo it. Too much activator can make your slime tough and not stretchy.

7. Mix in your plastic ocean toys and seashells for the perfect under the sea slime!

POPPIN' POPCORN SLIME

No, this slime isn't actually made with popcorn, but it sure looks like it is. And the crunching you hear when you play with it sounds like popcorn popping!

MATERIALS:

½ cup hot tap water

½ teaspoon baking soda

½ cup white PVA glue

5 drops yellow
food coloring

½ to 1 cup polystyrene
foam beads

2 to 3 tablespoons saline
solution containing
sodium borate
and boric acid

Measuring cup

Measuring spoons

Medium bowl

Mixing tools (spoons, craft
sticks, or a spatula)

SLIME SECRET: Instead of using foam beads in step 4, you can break up biodegradable packing peanuts into small pieces for the same popcorn effect.

WHAT YOU DO:

1. Combine the hot tap water and baking soda in a bowl and stir until the baking soda is completely dissolved.

2. Next add the clear PVA glue and mix well.

3. Add in the yellow food coloring and stir.

4. Now it's time to mix in the polystyrene foam beads. Start with ½ cup and stir well to incorporate all the beads. Mix in more foam beads depending on the consistency and look of the popcorn that you want.

5. Next, put in the saline solution a little at a time. Start by adding ½ tablespoon and stirring. Repeat until the mixture starts to clump up.

6. Mix until your slime begins taking on a ball-like form. It will begin coming off the sides of your bowl and sticking together.

7. Start kneading the slime with your hands. It will be very sticky at first, but as you continue to knead it, the slime will become less sticky and more solid. If it remains very sticky after kneading it a while, add in a teaspoon of saline solution at a time until you get your desired consistency. However, don't overdo it. Too much activator can make your slime tough and not stretchy.

SLIME SECRET: Can't find the perfect plastic beads? Use foam beads instead. They come in a variety of sizes and colors. Just add 2 tablespoons of colored foam beads in step 8 and knead them in.

OUT OF THIS GALAXY SLIME

● ● ● ●

Galaxy slime is very popular and can be found all over social media. I was inspired to create our version of the recipe after spotting perfect little "planets" in a craft store.

MATERIALS:

1½ cups hot tap water

1½ teaspoons baking soda

1½ cups clear PVA glue

4 to 5 drops black food coloring

4 tablespoons blue glitter

4 to 5 drops purple food coloring

4 to 5 drops blue food coloring

2 tablespoons silver glitter

6 to 9 tablespoons saline solution containing sodium borate and boric acid

Small, round colored beads

Measuring cup

Measuring spoons

Large bowl

3 medium bowls

Mixing tools (spoons, craft sticks, or a spatula)

WHAT YOU DO:

1. Combine the hot tap water and baking soda in a large bowl and stir until the baking soda is completely dissolved.

2. Next add the clear PVA glue and mix well. Then divide the mixture equally into 3 bowls.

3. In the first bowl, mix in the black food coloring and 2 tablespoons of blue glitter. In the second, mix in the purple food coloring and the rest of the blue glitter. In the third, mix in the blue food coloring and silver glitter.

4. Now, put in the saline solution a little at a time. Start by adding ½ tablespoon and stirring. Repeat until the mixture starts to clump up.

5. Mix until your slime begins coming off the sides of your bowl and forming into a ball.

6. Start kneading the slime with your hands. As you continue, the slime will become less sticky and more solid. If it remains very sticky, add in a teaspoon of saline solution at a time until you get your desired consistency.

7. Lay each slime side by side on a flat, protected surface and twist them together to make one slime.

8. Add colored beads to the mixture, and you'll have your very own galaxy!

MAGICAL UNICORN SLIME

Unicorn slime is usually made with pretty colors and lots of glitter. I like using pink, gold, and sparkly white for our recipe. But you can use whatever colors you like to create your own unique blend. After all, no two unicorns are alike!

MATERIALS:

1 batch Glitter Bomb
Slime (page 15)

1 cup hot tap water

1 teaspoon baking soda

1 cup white PVA glue

3 tablespoons gold glitter

5 drops pink food coloring

3 tablespoons
iridescent glitter

4 to 6 tablespoons saline
solution containing
sodium borate
and boric acid

Measuring cups

Measuring spoons

3 medium bowls

Mixing tools (spoons, craft
sticks, or a spatula)

WHAT YOU DO:

1. Make the Glitter Bomb Slime (page 15) using gold glitter instead of purple glitter and set aside.

2. In a new bowl, combine the hot tap water and baking soda, and stir until the baking soda is completely dissolved.

3. Next add the white PVA glue and mix well. Then evenly divide the mixture between 2 bowls.

4. Add the gold glitter to one bowl. Add the pink food coloring and iridescent glitter to the other bowl. Mix each thoroughly.

5. Begin stirring the saline solution into the pink mixture ½ tablespoon at a time. Repeat until the mixture starts to clump up. I normally use between 2 and 3 tablespoons of saline solution.

6. Mix until your slime begins taking on a ball-like form. It will begin coming off the sides of your bowl and sticking together.

7. Start kneading the slime with your hands. It will be very sticky at first, but as you continue to knead it, the slime will become less sticky and more solid. If it remains ➡

very sticky after kneading it a while, add in a teaspoon of saline solution at a time until you get your desired consistency. However, don't overdo it. Too much activator can make your slime tough and not stretchy.

8. Repeat steps 5 through 7 with the sparkly white mixture.

9. Now lay your 3 slimes side by side on a flat, protected surface. Twist them together to create one big glittery, magical slime!

STEP IT UP: Make special Unicorn Jars to give to friends!

HOW TO MAKE A UNICORN JAR

MATERIALS:

Baby food jar or small jar with a lid

Gold paint

White card stock paper

Gold glitter card stock paper

Decorative mini flowers

Paintbrush

Hot glue gun

WHAT YOU DO:

1. Paint the lid of a small jar gold. Set it aside to dry.

2. Make tiny unicorn ears by cutting two triangles from white card stock paper. For the horn, cut slightly a larger triangle out of gold glitter paper.

3. Ask an adult for help using the hot glue gun.

4. Glue the ears and horn onto your gold-painted lid. Then glue on the mini flowers.

5. Put some Magical Unicorn Slime into the jar and close the lid tightly.

6. Give it to a friend!

APPLE PIE JELLY CUBE SLIME

● ● ● ●

This Apple Pie Jelly Cube Slime is scented like apple pie and smells almost good enough to eat. Jelly cube slime is fun for squishing in your hands to create the satisfying crunching sounds we all love.

MATERIALS:

1 Magic Eraser sponge

½ cup hot tap water

½ teaspoon baking soda

½ cup clear PVA glue

4 to 5 drops brown food coloring

2 tablespoons gold glitter

2 to 3 drops apple pie scented oil

2 to 3 tablespoons saline solution containing sodium borate and boric acid

Scissors

Measuring cup

Measuring spoons

Medium bowl

Mixing tools (spoons, craft sticks, or a spatula)

WHAT YOU DO:

1. Using scissors, cut up a Magic Eraser sponge into small cubes and set aside.

2. Combine the hot tap water and baking soda in a bowl and stir until the baking soda is completely dissolved.

3. Next add the clear PVA glue, brown food coloring, gold glitter, and apple pie scented oil. Mix well.

4. Now, put in the saline solution a little at a time. Start by adding ½ tablespoon and stirring. Repeat until the mixture starts to clump up.

5. Mix until your slime begins taking on a ball-like form. It will begin coming off the sides of your bowl and sticking together.

6. Add the Magic Eraser sponge cubes.

7. Start kneading the slime with your hands. It will be very sticky at first, but as you continue to knead it, the slime will become less sticky and more solid. If it remains very sticky after kneading it a while, add in a teaspoon of saline solution at a time until you get your desired consistency. However, don't overdo it. Too much activator can make your slime tough and not stretchy.

SLIME SECRET: It is best to add the Magic Eraser sponge cubes while the slime is sticky so the pieces don't fall out. This recipe might require more activator to accommodate the pieces of sponge.

MYTHICAL MERMAID SLIME

● ● ● ●

I love making Mythical Mermaid Slime. The glossy blues with hints of purple and glitter remind me of the ocean. The sheen of the pearl pigment we use makes me think of the scales on a mermaid's tail.

MATERIALS:

1 cup hot tap water

1 teaspoon baking soda

1 cup clear PVA glue

2 tablespoons silver glitter

4 to 6 tablespoons saline solution containing sodium borate and boric acid

2 tablespoons purple pigment powder

2 tablespoons blue pearl pearl pigment powder

Measuring cup

Measuring spoons

2 medium bowls

Mixing tools (spoons, craft sticks, or a spatula)

WHAT YOU DO:

1. Combine the hot tap water and baking soda in a bowl and stir until the baking soda is completely dissolved.

2. Next add the clear PVA glue and silver glitter. Mix well.

3. Now, put in the saline solution a little at a time. Start by adding 1 tablespoon and stirring. Repeat until the mixture starts to clump up.

4. Mix until your slime begins taking on a ball-like form. It will begin coming off the sides of your bowl and sticking together.

5. Start kneading the slime with your hands. It will be very sticky at first, but as you continue to knead it, the slime will become less sticky and more solid. If it remains very sticky after kneading it a while, add in a teaspoon of saline solution at a time until you get your desired consistency. However, don't overdo it. Too much activator can make your slime tough and not stretchy.

6. Divide your slime into 2 bowls. In one bowl, use your finger to form a small indentation in the middle of your slime and pour in ½ tablespoon of purple pearl pigment powder. Fold the edges of your slime into the middle so that you knead the pigment powder into the slime. If you think your slime needs more pigment powder, add in 1 teaspoon at a time and fold and knead your slime to mix the pigment in. ➡

7. In the other bowl, follow the instructions in step 6 to add the blue pearl pigment powder.

8. Lay your slimes side by side on a flat, protected surface. Twist them together to create one big mermaid slime!

STEP IT UP: You can customize this mermaid slime any way you like, with things such as chunky pieces of sequins or fishbowl beads. These will change the look and texture of the slime.

BIRTHDAY CAKE BUTTER SLIME

This Birthday Cake Butter Slime is very satisfying to play with, and it smells delicious. It's not taste-safe, though, so don't eat it.

MATERIALS:

½ cup hot tap water

½ teaspoon baking soda

½ cup white PVA glue

3 drops cake batter scented oil

2 to 3 tablespoons saline solution containing sodium borate and boric acid

3 ounces white Crayola Model Magic air-dry clay

3 tablespoons rainbow foam beads

Measuring cup

Measuring spoons

Medium bowl

Mixing tools (spoons, craft sticks, or a spatula)

WHAT YOU DO:

1. Combine the hot tap water and baking soda in a bowl and stir until the baking soda is completely dissolved.

2. Next add the white PVA glue and cake batter scented oil. Mix well.

3. Now, put in the saline solution a little at a time. Start by adding ½ tablespoon and. Repeat until the mixture starts to clump up.

4. Mix until your slime begins taking on a ball-like form. It will begin coming off the sides of your bowl and sticking together.

5. Start kneading the slime with your hands. It will be very sticky at first, but as you continue to knead it, the slime will become less sticky and more solid. If it remains very sticky after kneading it a while, add in a teaspoon of saline solution at a time until you get your desired consistency. However, don't overdo it. Too much activator can make your slime tough and not stretchy.

6. Next add the white Crayola Model Magic air-dry clay. Knead and pull until it's thoroughly mixed in with your slime. This will take a few minutes.

7. Once you're done, top with the rainbow foam beads. These will look like sprinkles on the slime cake!

STEP IT UP: Have a Birthday Cake Butter Slime making contest for fun at your next birthday party.

SLIME SECRET: Too much instant snow will make your slime crumbly. If this happens, add ¼ cup of Basic Slime (page 11) until you get the desired consistency.

COTTON CANDY FLUFF 'N' STUFF

● ● ● ●

The texture of cloud slime is cool, but when you add in cotton candy colors and scents, it makes it so much better!

MATERIALS:

1 cup hot tap water

1 teaspoon baking soda

1 cup white PVA glue

3 drops cotton candy scented oil

3 drops blue food coloring

3 drops pink food coloring

4 to 6 tablespoons saline solution containing sodium borate and boric acid

½ cup instant snow, made according to package instructions

Measuring cup

Measuring spoons

2 medium bowls

Mixing tools (spoons, craft sticks, or a spatula)

WHAT YOU DO:

1. Combine the hot tap water and baking soda in a bowl and stir until the baking soda is completely dissolved.

2. Next add the white PVA glue and cotton candy scented oil. Mix well.

3. Evenly divide the mixture into 2 bowls. Add the blue food coloring to one bowl and the pink to the other.

4. Now, put in the saline solution a little at a time. Start by adding ½ tablespoon to the blue mixture and stirring. Repeat until the mixture starts to clump up.

5. Mix until your slime begins coming off the sides of your bowl and forming into a ball.

6. Start kneading the slime with your hands. It will be very sticky at first, but as you continue to knead it, the slime will become less sticky and more solid. If it remains very sticky after kneading it a while, add in a teaspoon of saline solution at a time until you get your desired consistency. However, don't overdo it. Too much activator can make your slime tough and not stretchy.

7. Repeat steps 4 through 6 for the pink mixture.

8. Mix ¼ cup of instant snow (made according to package instructions) into each batch of slime.

9. Lay your slimes side by side on a flat, protected surface. Then twist them together to create one cloud of slime that looks like cotton candy!

RAINBOW FOIL SLIME

Gold leaf foil adds a fun pop of shine to the rainbow colors in this slime recipe. Once the foil breaks up, it almost looks like chunks of confetti.

MATERIALS:

2 cups hot tap water

2 teaspoons baking soda

2 cups white PVA glue

3 drops pink food coloring

3 drops green food coloring

3 drops blue food coloring

3 drops orange food coloring

8 to 12 tablespoons saline solution containing sodium borate and boric acid

1 to 2 sheets gold leaf foil (any color)

Measuring cup

Measuring spoons

Lareg bowl

4 medium bowls

Mixing tools (spoons, craft sticks, or a spatula)

SLIME SECRET: Rainbow-colored foil adds an extra pop to this recipe.

WHAT YOU DO:

1. Combine the hot tap water and baking soda in a large bowl, and stir until the baking soda is completely dissolved.

2. Next add the white PVA glue and mix well.

3. Now, evenly divide the mixture into 4 medium bowls. Add the pink food coloring to the first bowl, green to the second, blue to the third, and orange to the fourth.

4. Begin stirring the saline solution ½ tablespoon at a time into the pink mixture. Repeat until the mixture starts to clump up. I normally use between 2 and 3 tablespoons of saline solution.

5. Mix until your slime begins taking on a ball-like form. It will begin coming off the sides of your bowl and sticking together.

6. Start kneading the slime with your hands. It will be very sticky at first, but as you continue to knead it, the slime will become less sticky and more solid. If it remains very sticky after kneading it a while, add in a teaspoon of saline solution at a time until you get your desired consistency. However, don't overdo it.

7. Repeat steps 4 through 6 to make the green, blue, and orange slimes.

8. Lay your 4 slimes side by side on a flat, protected surface. Then add in the colored foil.

KINETIC SLIME

● ● ● ●

Have you ever thought of putting sand in slime? You can use beach sand, or you can try store-bought kinetic sand. Kinetic sand gives slime a moldable texture that my kids and I love! It feels like slime, but it oozes a little more slowly.

MATERIALS:

½ cup hot tap water

½ teaspoon baking soda

½ cup white PVA glue

2 to 3 tablespoons saline solution containing sodium borate and boric acid

½ cup pink kinetic sand

Measuring cup

Measuring spoons

Medium bowl

Mixing tools (spoons, craft sticks, or a spatula)

SLIME SECRET: Use colored kinetic sand instead of trying to color your slime with food coloring.

WHAT YOU DO:

1. Combine the hot tap water and baking soda in a bowl and stir until the baking soda is completely dissolved.

2. Next add the white PVA glue and mix well.

3. Now, put in the saline solution a little at a time. Start by adding ½ tablespoon and stirring. Repeat until the mixture starts to clump up.

4. Mix until your slime begins taking on a ball-like form. It will begin coming off the sides of your bowl and sticking together.

5. Start kneading the slime with your hands. It will be very sticky at first, but as you continue to knead it, the slime will become less sticky and more solid. If it remains very sticky after kneading it a while, add in a teaspoon of saline solution at a time until you get your desired consistency. However, don't overdo it. Too much activator can make your slime tough and not stretchy, and the sand will make your slime harder once it's added.

6. Add the pink kinetic sand and knead it into the slime. If the sand makes your slime sticky, add in ½ teaspoon of saline solution at a time and knead until it is no longer sticky.

AVALANCHE SLIME

● ● ● ●

Avalanche slime is unique. Each one you make will look totally different. For this recipe, you'll be making two different kinds of clear slime and a basic white slime. The "avalanche" forms when the white slime settles into the colored clear slimes on the bottom of a container. It's such a cool effect, and I can see why it's so popular on social media. Let's try it!

MATERIALS:

1 batch Basic Slime with white glue (page 11)

1 cup hot tap water

1 teaspoon baking soda

1 cup clear PVA glue

3 drops blue food coloring

3 drops purple food coloring

4 to 6 tablespoons saline solution containing sodium borate and boric acid

Measuring cup

Measuring spoons

3 medium bowls

Mixing tools (spoons, craft sticks, or a spatula)

1 medium clear container (holds about 8 cups)

WHAT YOU DO:

1. In a separate bowl, combine the hot tap water and baking soda, and stir until the baking soda is completely dissolved.

2. Next add the clear PVA glue and mix well.

3. Now, evenly divide the mixture into 2 bowls. Add the blue food coloring to one bowl and the purple food coloring to the other.

4. Begin stirring the saline solution into the blue mixture ½ tablespoon at a time. Repeat until the mixture starts to clump up. I normally use between 2 and 3 tablespoons of saline solution.

5. Mix until your slime begins taking on a ball-like form. It will begin coming off the sides of your bowl and sticking together.

6. Start kneading the slime with your hands. It will be very sticky at first, but as you continue to knead it, the slime will become less sticky and more solid. If it remains very sticky after kneading it a while, add in a teaspoon of saline solution at a time until you get your desired consistency. However, don't overdo it. Too much activator can make your slime tough and not stretchy. ➡

7. Wash your hands, then repeat steps 5 through 7 with the purple mixture.

8. Now that your 3 slimes are ready, it's time to make the avalanche!

TO MAKE THE AVALANCHE:

1. Place the clear blue slime on the bottom of one side of the container. Then place the clear purple slime next to it. Make sure you press the two slimes into the bottom of the container to make room for the white slime.

2. Add the white slime on top of the blue and purple slimes. Then put the lid on the container to seal it up.

3. Let the slime sit for at least 24 hours. The larger the container is, the longer it will take for the avalanche to happen.

SLIME SECRET: You can make Avalanche Slime with any color of clear slime—even glittery colors—but always use white slime for the top. Think of it as the snow in your avalanche!

SLIME SCIENTIST:
YOUR VERY OWN SLIMES

• • • •

Now that you've learned how to transform a basic slime recipe into something amazing and eye-catching, it's time to design your own. In this chapter, I'm going to help you get creative and have fun with making your own slime recipes.

GET CREATIVE

One of the reasons I love making and playing with slime is that it's such a great tool to learn more about science. It's also great for helping manage anxiety and stress. There's just something about playing with squishy and stretchy things. You can stretch it and knead it like dough or fold it over and pop it like putty. Making and playing with slime is a relaxing and calming activity.

This chapter is going to start you off with a basic slime procedure that you can follow to create and test new recipes. It's important to always remember that anything you add into your slime will have an impact on how it feels and flows. As you become more familiar with the basic slime recipes and as your knowledge of slime grows, you'll begin to understand which product is necessary to achieve a desired effect.

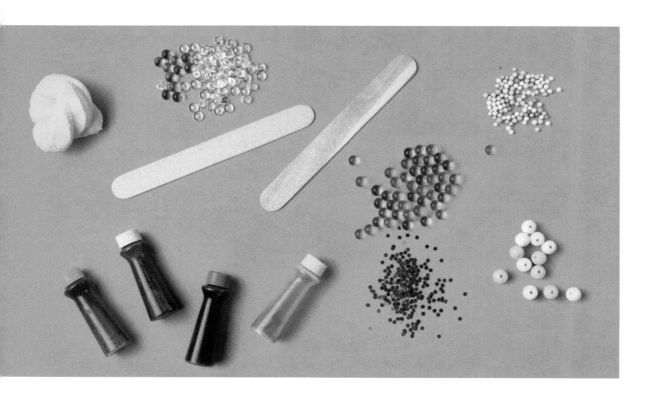

SLIME SECRET: SOLVE YOUR SLIME PROBLEMS

Before we get into how to make your own slimes, I want to share some tips and tricks that my kids and I have learned along our slime journey:

- **FIXING HARD SLIME:** If your slime is feeling too dry and cakey, simply mix 1 teaspoon of lotion into your slime. If it's still too hard, add in another 1 teaspoon until your slime is as good as new!

- **FIXING WATERY SLIME:** The easiest way to fix slime that's too loose is to mix in 1 teaspoon of saline solution at a time until you get your desired consistency.

- **FIXING STRINGY SLIME:** You may not have kneaded the slime enough. Keep kneading.

- **FIXING THICK OR TOUGH SLIME:** Knead ½ tablespoon of lotion into your slime. Continue this until you get your desired consistency.

- **REMOVING SLIME FROM HAIR:** First, don't panic! Instead of opting for a new haircut, rub lemon juice on the slime in your hair. The juice will make the slime melt. Once the slime is removed, wash your hair.

- **REMOVING SLIME FROM CLOTHES:** Vinegar is your best friend when it comes to slime stains. Try to wipe off as much of the slime as possible, and as soon as possible. Then soak the stain in vinegar and scrub. Once you've scrubbed the stain clean, you can put the clothes in the wash.

- **OOPS! FORGOT TO BUY COLOR ADD-INS?** Color the top of the slime with a felt tip marker. Then knead the slime to mix the color through.

- **WANT JEWEL-TONED SLIME?** Use clear glue.

- **WANT BRIGHT SLIME?** Use white glue.

- **WANT SUPER-DUPER STRETCHY SLIME?** Switch out the water in your basic slime recipe for bubble solution.

- **WANT TO MAKE LOTS OF SLIME?** Buy the big jugs of glue. The little bottles won't last for much more than one recipe.

CHOOSE YOUR SLIME STYLE

First, you need to choose what type of slime to make. Do you want it soft and buttery, crunchy and not as stretchy, or super stretchy? Do you want it to be sparkly, cloudy, or spongy? Here's a chart that you can pair with the basic slime recipe to achieve the kind of slime you want to make. Don't be afraid of a slime fail—that's an important part of learning and having fun!

TYPE	ADD-IN	BENEFIT	CHALLENGE
CRUNCHY SLIME	Fishbowl beads, pony beads, or sequins	Satisfying crunchy sound and texture	Not as stretchy
FLUFFY SLIME	Shaving cream or hair mousse	Very soft, smooth, and stretchy	Too much shaving cream can make the slime too hard
METALLIC SLIME	Metallic paint or metallic pigment powder	Very shiny and stretchy, a great base recipe for outer space slime	Using too many metallic colors can make it turn brown
BUTTER SLIME	Model Magic air-dry clay	Super-soft and shiny texture	Will dry out if left out too long
FLOAM SLIME	Polystyrene foam beads or biodegradable packing peanuts	Crunchy sound and texture	If you add too many foam beads they'll fall out, and too many can make the slime stiff
GLOW-IN-THE-DARK SLIME	Glow-in-the-dark glue or phosphorescent powder	Creates a glow-in-the-dark effect and is still stretchy	You have to recharge your slime by a light to get it to continue to glow
CLOUD SLIME	Instant snow	Creates a soft, cloudlike texture	Can be messy measuring out the instant snow
JELLY CUBE SLIME	Magic Erasers	Creates a thick popping and crunching sound when played with	Can be harder to stretch depending on how many sponges you put in

BUILD YOUR RECIPE

After you've figured out what style of slime you want to make, you'll have an idea of what type of base you want to use. For example, for a buttery soft slime with creamy texture you want a basic white slime recipe, and for a slime that looks clear blue like the ocean you want a slime like Under the Sea Slime (page 53).

When creating different effects, try not to add too many colors and textures. The key to a good slime is to keep it simple. When you mix too many things together, it can get too busy and end up turning your slime hard in texture or even brown in color. Start with simple combinations and then add things to make them more complex.

SLIME SECRET: MORE SLIME DOS AND DON'TS

DO:

- **ADD** your own favorite items to your slime to make it unique.
- **FOLLOW** the basic slime steps in the correct order.
- **USE** saline solution with sodium borate and boric acid in it.
- **KNOW** what perfect slime looks like. It holds together and doesn't have any visible strings of glue. When you grab it, it moves as one cohesive unit.

DON'T:

- **USE** dollar store glue. The most common reason for slime gone wrong is the wrong type of glue. Make sure you use quality glue with the ingredient PVA; otherwise, your slime will be soup.
- **SUBSTITUTE** for key ingredients.
- **ADD** all of your activator at once. If you do, your slime won't be stretchy and will remain too sticky.
- **APPROXIMATE** measurements, especially if you're new to making slime.

TEST YOUR SLIME

Here are some steps you can follow to test your slime. It is important to write down everything you are putting into your slime so you can figure out why your creations are or aren't working correctly. The Slime Diary (page 87) is the perfect place for this information.

1. Start by following along with this basic step to design your slime:
    *   Glue (clear or white)
    *   Activator (avoid borax and choose a safer option like saline solution)
    *   Coloring (pigments, paints, food coloring, etc.)
    *   Add-ins (beads, glitter, sequins, etc.)
    *   Scents (essential oils or even flavored extracts work well)

2. Then record all of your ingredients, measurements, and methods so that you have a record of what you tried.

3. Make a hypothesis: How do you think your slime will turn out? Will it be soft and fluffy, stretchy, or stiff and crunchy?

4. Then make the slime and record your results. Did you get what you expected? If not, what do you think went wrong? How could you improve the experiment?

5. If your slime is a fail, double-check that your measurements are correct with the base slime recipe you used. Then check the Dos and Don'ts (page 85) and Slime Secret: Solve Your Slime Problems (page 83).

SLIME DIARY

• • • •

Use the following pages to keep track of your
slime experiments—just like a scientist. Record ingredients
and recipes, note your thoughts and observations,
and mark the results of your creations!

SLIME DIARY

◯ Success ◯ Fail

SLIME NAME: ______________________________

INGREDIENTS USED:

______________________ ______________________

______________________ ______________________

______________________ ______________________

______________________ ______________________

HOW TO IMPROVE IT:

____

____

____

____

____

OTHER NOTES:

____

____

____

____

____

____

◯ Success ◯ Fail

SLIME NAME: _____

INGREDIENTS
USED: _____ _____

_____ _____

_____ _____

_____ _____

HOW TO
IMPROVE IT: _____

_____

_____

_____

_____

_____

OTHER
NOTES: _____

_____

_____

_____

_____

_____

◯ Success ◯ Fail

SLIME NAME: _____

INGREDIENTS USED: _____ _____

_____ _____

_____ _____

_____ _____

HOW TO IMPROVE IT: _____

_____

_____

_____

_____

_____

OTHER NOTES: _____

_____

_____

_____

_____

_____

◯ Success   ◯ Fail

SLIME NAME: _____

INGREDIENTS USED: _____ _____

_____ _____

_____ _____

_____ _____

HOW TO IMPROVE IT: _____

_____

_____

_____

_____

OTHER NOTES: _____

_____

_____

_____

_____

_____

◯ Success ◯ Fail

SLIME NAME: _____

INGREDIENTS USED: _____ _____

_____ _____

_____ _____

_____ _____

HOW TO IMPROVE IT: _____

_____

_____

_____

_____

OTHER NOTES: _____

_____

_____

_____

_____

◯ Success ◯ Fail

SLIME DIARY

SLIME NAME: ______________________

INGREDIENTS USED: ______________________

HOW TO IMPROVE IT: ______________________

OTHER NOTES: ______________________

◯ Success   ◯ Fail

SLIME NAME: _____

INGREDIENTS
USED: _____   _____

_____   _____

_____   _____

_____   _____

HOW TO
IMPROVE IT: _____

_____

_____

_____

_____

OTHER
NOTES: _____

_____

_____

_____

_____

_____

◯ Success   ◯ Fail

SLIME NAME: _____

INGREDIENTS
USED: _____   _____

_____   _____

_____   _____

_____   _____

HOW TO
IMPROVE IT: _____

_____

_____

_____

_____

OTHER
NOTES: _____

_____

_____

_____

_____

◯ Success   ◯ Fail

SLIME NAME: _____

INGREDIENTS USED: _____   _____
_____   _____
_____   _____
_____   _____

HOW TO IMPROVE IT: _____
_____
_____
_____
_____
_____

OTHER NOTES: _____
_____
_____
_____
_____
_____

◯ Success   ◯ Fail

SLIME NAME: _____

INGREDIENTS
USED: _____   _____

_____   _____

_____   _____

_____   _____

HOW TO
IMPROVE IT: _____

_____

_____

_____

_____

_____

OTHER
NOTES: _____

_____

_____

_____

_____

_____

_____

SLIME DIARY

◯ Success ◯ Fail

SLIME NAME: ________________________________

INGREDIENTS USED: ________________ ________________

________________ ________________

________________ ________________

________________ ________________

HOW TO IMPROVE IT: ________________________________

____

____

____

____

OTHER NOTES: ________________________________

____

____

____

____

____

INDEX

● ● ● ●

ACKNOWLEDGMENTS

●●●●

WITHOUT MY FAMILY, this book wouldn't exist. Thank you to my little slimers, Jace and Aria. They're the creative minds and slime testers behind all of these oozy, gooey creations. And thank you to my husband, who has encouraged my love of the arts and puts up with all the glitter, glue, and creative mess that accompanies it.

ABOUT THE AUTHOR

● ● ● ●

JACKIE HOUSTON is the founder of iHeartArtsnCrafts.com. Founded in 2014, *I Heart Arts 'n' Crafts* was created to bring to parents simple and fun ideas for hands-on activities, kids' crafts, and messy play. She promotes learning, creativity, simplicity, and most of all fun! When she doesn't have her hands covered in glitter and glue, you can find her at baseball games and dance lessons with her kids in Pittsburgh, Pennsylvania.

CPSIA information can be obtained
at www.ICGtesting.com
Printed in the USA
BVHW051507140219
540186BV00002B/2